Peter Rabbit's ABC and 123

With new reproductions from the original illustrations

BY BEATRIX POTTER

F. WARNE & Co

Aa

a is for apples

Red and green apples,
in a big brown pot

b is for butter

Samuel Whiskers is
stealing the butter!

Cc

c is for carrot

This rabbit's mother has
given him a carrot

d is for duck

Can you make a
noise like a duck?

E e

e is for egg

A present of an egg
for Mr Brown

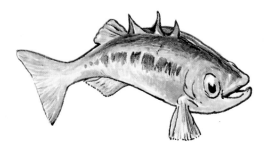

f is for fish

Splash! Jack Sharp,
covered in spines

Gg

g is for gate

Look at naughty Peter Rabbit,
squeezing under the gate

h is for hedgehog

Mrs Tiggy-winkle
is nothing but a hedgehog!

i is for iron

Mrs Tiggy-winkle ironing,
makes a nice hot singey smell

j is for jacket

Jj

Peter Rabbit's jacket,
hanging on the scarecrow

Kk

k is for kitten

Mittens, Tom Kitten and Moppet,
playing in the garden

Ll

l is for ladybird

"Fly away home,
Mother Ladybird!"

Mm

m is for mouse

A little mouse, on top
of the cupboard

n is for newspaper

The foxy-gentleman looks over
the top of his newspaper

O o

o is for owl

Can you make a noise
like an owl?

p is for pig

This little pig went to market;
his name is Pigling Bland

Qq

q is for quilt

Little baby mice,
sleeping all in a row

Rr

r is for rabbits

Can you see the little
bunny, peeping over?

S s

s is for strawberry

Timmy Willie eats roots and salad
(and sometimes a strawberry)

T t

t is for teacup

Simpkin the cat
was fond of mice

Uu

u is for umbrella

Timmy and Goody Tiptoes,
under an umbrella

V v

v is for violets

Timmy Willie sits in the sun,
sniffing the smell of violets

W w

w is for washing

Mrs Tiggy-winkle,
hanging up her washing

Xx

x is in fox

Jemima Puddle-duck
meets a foxy-gentleman

Y y

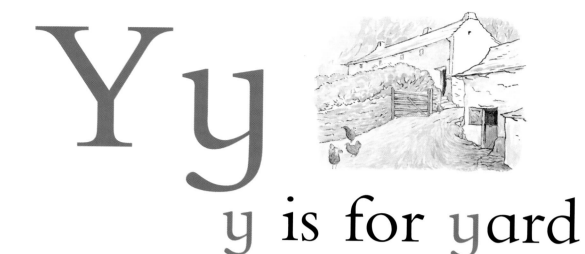

y is for yard

Lucie is in the farm-yard,
looking for her pocket-handkins

z is for "Zzz, bizz"

Can you make a noise
like a bee?

1

one rabbit

How many little rabbits,
eating radishes?

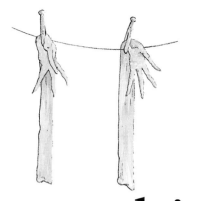

two stockings

How many yellow stockings
for Sally Henny-penny?

3

three kittens

One, two, three little kittens,
playing in the dust

four guinea-pigs 4

How many guinea-pigs can
you see in the garden?

5

five mice

How many mice sewing,
with scissors and thread?

six rabbits

How many Flopsy Bunnies,
peeping in the window?

7

seven **squirrels**

Can you count the red squirrels
with the old brown owl?

8

eight piglets

How many piglets, feeding from a trough?

9

nine mice

Can you count the mice,
sitting up for supper?

10
ten **mice**

How many little mice,
living in a shoe?

11

eleven **hens**

How many hens
in the hen coop?

twelve **animals**

The "PETER RABBIT" BOOKS
by BEATRIX POTTER

PETER RABBIT · SQUIRREL NUTKIN
TAILOR OF GLOUCESTER · BENJAMIN BUNNY
TWO BAD MICE · MRS. TIGGY-WINKLE
MR. JEREMY FISHER · TOM KITTEN
JEMIMA PUDDLE-DUCK · THE FLOPSY BUNNIES
MRS. TITTLEMOUSE · TIMMY TIPTOES
JOHNNY TOWN-MOUSE · MR. TOD
PIGLING BLAND · SAMUEL WHISKERS
THE PIE & THE PATTY-PAN · GINGER & PICKLES
LITTLE PIG ROBINSON

A FIERCE BAD RABBIT   MISS MOPPET
APPLEY DAPPLY'S   CECILY PARSLEY'S
NURSERY RHYMES   NURSERY RHYMES
PETER RABBIT'S   TOM KITTEN'S
PAINTING BOOK   PAINTING BOOK

How many animals
round the notice-board?

FREDERICK WARNE

Published by the Penguin Group
27 Wrights Lane, London W8 5TZ, England
Penguin Books USA Inc., 375 Hudson Street, New York, New York 10014, USA
Penguin Books Australia Ltd, Ringwood, Victoria, Australia
Penguin Books Canada Ltd, 10 Alcorn Avenue, Toronto, Ontario, Canada M4V 3B2
Penguin Books (NZ) Ltd, 182-190 Wairau Road, Auckland 10, New Zealand

Penguin Books Ltd, Registered Offices: Harmondsworth, Middlesex, England

First published in 1995
5 7 9 10 8 6

ISBN 07232 4188 0

Colour reproduction by
Saxon Photolitho Ltd, Norwich
Printed and bound in Great Britain by
William Clowes Limited, Beccles and London